THE MARCUS RASHFORD

YOU ARE A CHAMPION ACTION PLANNER

50 Activities to Achieve Your Dreams

OTHER BOOKS BY MARCUS RASHFORD

You Are a Champion
Written with Carl Anka

You Can Do It
Written with Carl Anka

The Breakfast Club Adventures:
The Beast Beyond the Fence
Written with Alex Falase-Koya

THE MARCUS RASHFORD

YOU ARE A CHAMPION ACTION PLANNER

Written with
Katie Warriner
and Carl Anka

50 ACTIVITIES TO ACHIEVE YOUR DREAMS

MACMILLAN CHILDREN'S BOOKS

Published 2022 by Macmillan Children's Books
an imprint of Pan Macmillan
The Smithson, 6 Briset Street, London EC1M 5NR
EU representative: Macmillan Publishers Ireland Ltd, 1st Floor,
The Liffey Trust Centre, 117–126 Sheriff Street Upper
Dublin 1, D01 YC43
Associated companies throughout the world
www.panmacmillan.com

ISBN 978-1-0350-1404-0

1 3 5 7 9 8 6 4 2

A CIP catalogue record for this book is available from the British Library.

Printed and bound by CPI Group (UK) Ltd, Croydon CR0 4YY
Designed by Janene Spencer

Credits
Mental Muscle Activity on p56 based on the Kind and Caring Coach exercise, adapted from *Act for Treating Children*
by Tamar D. Black copyright © Tamar D. Black 2022, used by permission of New Harbinger Publications exercise.

Graphic on p131 © Moonshot Series Ltd. www.moonshotseries.co.uk

CONTENTS

HI THERE, AND WELCOME TO YOUR ACTION PLANNER!

(I know, I know — it's got 'planner' in the name. But don't worry, this will be a bit different from the usual textbooks you get at school. Trust me!)

If you've read my book *You Are a Champion* you'll know that one thing I like about books, is that everyone can take something different from them. I like to go back to my favourite books at different times in the year because I find myself learning new things from different sections. I want to give that experience to **YOU**, so that's why I've created this action planner that you're holding in your hands.

I WANT THIS BOOK TO HELP YOU MANAGE LIFE'S UPS AND DOWNS, DISCOVER YOUR POTENTIAL AND BE THE BEST YOU CAN BE. WHEREVER YOU ARE ON YOUR LIFE'S JOURNEY, AND WHATEVER IS GOING ON FOR YOU RIGHT NOW, I'M REALLY HAPPY THAT YOU'VE OPENED THIS BOOK.

And I want you to know that even if you haven't had the chance to read **You Are a Champion**, this book is still for you.

In **You Are a Champion** I shared lots of advice and stories from my own life to try and help you on your journey. In this book we're going to do something different — I'm going to share more stories and ideas with you, and there's also lots of space for you to write your own ideas down, so that you can create something that **YOU** can get the most out of.

THIS BOOK IS ABOUT YOU AND ONLY YOU CAN MAKE IT YOUR OWN

Before we go any further, I've got quite a big question for you.

Have you ever thought about how unique you are? I mean, think about what the chances were of you even being born! As in, you, at the exact time you were born, with your exact eye colour, height, skin colour, likes, dislikes, hopes, doubts and dreams . . . everything that makes you, **YOU!** Think about everything that had to happen for you to be you, exactly as you are!

TO HELP YOU THINK ABOUT THIS QUESTION, HERE ARE SOME FUN FACTS:

★ The chances of you being born with 11 fingers or toes = **1 in 500.** This means if you go to school with 500 people, one person might have been born with an extra finger or toe!

★ The chances of you being injured by a toilet = **1 in 10,000!**

★ The chances of you winning an Olympic medal = **1 in 662,000!**

★ The chances of you winning the lottery jackpot = **1 in 292 million!**

Scientists say the chance of you being born is about 1 in 400 trillion.

That's
FOUR HUNDRED TRILLION.
It has 12 zeros.

I'm going to write it out for you. And whenever you get a bit stuck, I want you to write the same thing too:

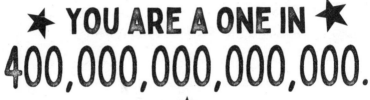

★ YOU ARE A ONE IN ★
400,000,000,000,000.

★
WHICH BASICALLY MEANS THAT
★ YOU'RE KIND OF A MIRACLE. ★

A MIRACLE IS AN EVENT SO UNLIKELY AS TO BE ALMOST IMPOSSIBLE.

I want you to make the most of that miracle, and this workbook is going to play a small part in helping you do that.

Throughout this book, I'm going to share lots of activities and questions with you to help you build something I call

MENTAL MUSCLE

MENTAL MUSCLE will help you achieve your dreams. It is all about knowing yourself, doing the best you can and giving you the tools you need to help you through when times get tough. It will help you discover how to be the best you can be. And just like all muscles, the more you practise, the stronger it will get, and the more cool stuff you can do with it!

The fact that you're where you are today proves that you already have a lot of **MENTAL MUSCLE!** Turn the page for an activity to get you thinking about the mental muscle you've already built:

MENTAL MUSCLE BAROMETER:

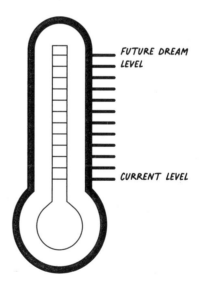

FUTURE DREAM LEVEL

CURRENT LEVEL

1. Write down something you're proud of. It could be a skill you have, or a competition you've won. It could even be something you've made — it can be anything!

_____

_____

_____

2. Write down a time where you faced your fears. (When I was younger the dog down the street used to freak me out, but over time I learned not to find it too scary.)

_____

_____

_____

_____

3. Write down a time when you could have given up but kept on trying. For me, that was practising my football skills, even though I found a lot of them hard.

_____

_____

_____

_____

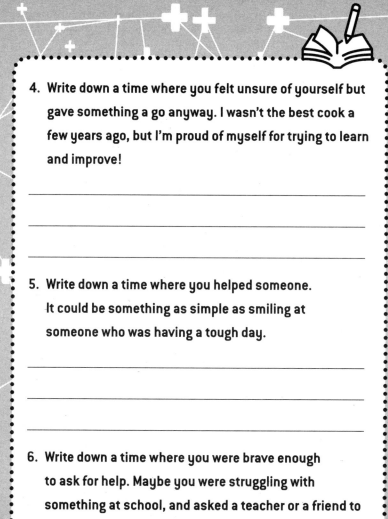

4. Write down a time where you felt unsure of yourself but gave something a go anyway. I wasn't the best cook a few years ago, but I'm proud of myself for trying to learn and improve!

_____

_____

_____

5. Write down a time where you helped someone. It could be something as simple as smiling at someone who was having a tough day.

_____

_____

_____

6. Write down a time where you were brave enough to ask for help. Maybe you were struggling with something at school, and asked a teacher or a friend to help you.

_____

_____

_____

The fact that you answered those questions proves that you already have TONS of **MENTAL MUSCLE.** But it doesn't matter where you're starting from, I'm just excited to help you build your **MENTAL MUSCLE** from here. Then you can use it to be the person you want to be and set out to achieve your dreams.

By the time you get to the end of this book, it's going to be full of things that no other version of this book will have. The front cover may look the same as an action planner owned by one of your friends, or someone else you know, but the stuff inside? That will be a bit different to everyone else.

YOUR ACTION PLANNER, JUST LIKE YOUR LIFE, IS COMPLETELY UNIQUE, AND THAT'S WHAT MAKES IT SPECIAL.

You might be wondering how to make this your **BEST** life ever? If so, I have a few words of wisdom. It makes me smile writing that because I don't think of myself as particularly wise, but when it comes to working on myself and trying to be the best I can be, I've learnt a lot over the years:

- ★ **WORK HARD**
- ★ **BE PATIENT WITH YOURSELF AND STICK WITH IT**
- ★ **BE HONEST**
- ★ **BE BRAVE**
- ★ **HAVE FUN**

Throughout this book, I'm going to ask you lots of questions and give you lots of activities to try. Some you'll love, some you might not be so sure on, but the most important thing is that you give them a go. Sometimes building **MENTAL MUSCLE** is fun and sometimes it's hard, but what you'll be able to do with that muscle will be **AMAZING!**

Take your time to read each page, share your ideas with friends and family and don't forget to be proud of yourself for giving it a go.

READY TO MAKE A START? LET'S GO!

M.R.

FIND YOUR
DREAM

Dreams allow us to express ourselves and discover what we're capable of.

SOME DREAMS HAVE THE POWER TO CHANGE YOUR LIFE, AND OTHERS CAN CHANGE THE WORLD.

Your dreams, just like you, are totally unique. They might be about following your passion, helping others, taking care of the planet or even making the next big discovery that changes the world! It can be as big or as small as you'd like and I'm here to help you find it.

SO, WHERE SHALL WE START?

I want you to imagine you're sitting in a room by yourself. In the room there is a table, a chair and a button. If you press the button, you will get an electric shock — the shock won't be too bad, but it won't feel nice. Your challenge is simply to sit in the room for 5 minutes. No phones, books, or posters to read.

Do you think you'd be able to do it?

YES ☐   NO ☐

People have actually been put in this situation for real, and the results are incredible! Over half the people in the experiment pressed the button to get an electric shock — one person pressed it over 100 times in 15 minutes! They found sitting in silence really hard, and would rather press the button — and get a nasty shock each time — for something to do!

OUR LIVES ARE SO BUSY AND WE'RE ALWAYS BEING GIVEN NEW INFORMATION — IF YOUR MIND IS ANYTHING LIKE MINE, IT CAN GET A BIT BUSY UP THERE. BUT IT'S IMPORTANT TO MAKE SPACE FOR QUIET, SO THAT YOU CAN SPEND SOME TIME THINKING ABOUT WHAT'S IMPORTANT TO YOU.

I like to think of my mind like a big lake, and all of my ideas are the fish that live in the water. When there's loads of noise and movement on the surface, some of the fish retreat and decide to stay deep in the water. But when things are calm, then some of the bigger fish travel up to the surface where you can see them.

If I make space in my mind for calm, I can surprise myself with the ideas I end up seeing. Some of my biggest dreams have come to me in these quiet moments, when my mind is relaxed and I've given it space to think.

YOU HAVE AMAZING DREAMS AND IDEAS IN YOUR HEAD TOO

— about how you want to live your life, what you want to achieve or the impact you want to have on others. Dreams are so important as they let you imagine a world where anything is possible, where you can look at things in different ways and achieve anything you put your mind to.

I want to help you make sure you're not too busy being distracted by other things to let those ideas come to the surface. Your brain needs down-time to ask great questions of yourself, and come up with great ideas.

SO, TIME FOR YOU TO HAVE A GO.

Get a timer, set it for 5 minutes and get rid of any distractions, like music or the TV. Sit comfortably. (This could be on the floor, or on the sofa, or on a bed – wherever you'd like!) I want you to stay like this, just sitting as you are, for 5 minutes.

You can either sit quietly and just see what happens in your mind, or, if you want something to focus on, pick a question you like from this list:

★ **Imagine you are the boss of Planet Earth. What would you like life to be like for the people who live there?**

★ **If you had a magic wand, what would you change?**

★ **What do you care about?**

★ **What makes you happy?**

★ **What do you want to achieve?**

Close your eyes if you want to. Start your timer, and go – just sit in silence and be with yourself!

DID YOU DO IT? DID YOU MANAGE TO SIT STILL FOR THE FULL 5 MINUTES? OR DID YOU GET DISTRACTED?

If you got distracted for a bit don't worry – that's completely normal and it happens to us all. If you're anything like me, your mind might be going something like this:

- ✱ I'm doing the activity and thinking about what I care about.
- ✱ Then my mind wanders to 'What's for dinner?' or 'This is a bit random isn't it?'
- ✱ I notice my mind has wandered.
- ✱ I take a deep breath and gently bring my focus back to the activity.

Getting distracted just shows that you have an opportunity to build your **MENTAL MUSCLE**.

I'd like you to try doing this activity again tomorrow, and the next day too. Each time you do it you'll notice your mind wandering, but that's ok. All you have to do is bring your attention back to your breathing, and the question you're thinking about. The more you practise, the more you'll be able let your bigger thoughts – like your hopes and dreams – come to the surface.

Take a look at the drawing below – it shows you that something amazing can be made of being still, noticing when you've been distracted and gently bringing your mind back to what you want to focus on.

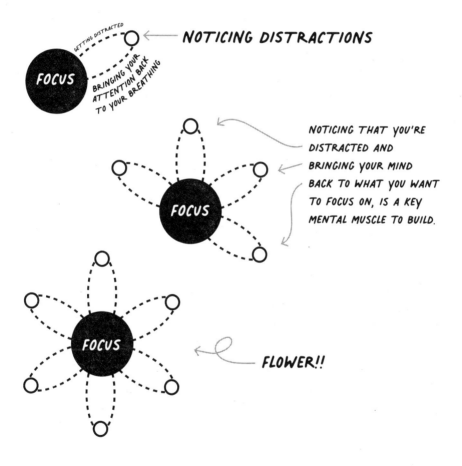

NOTICING DISTRACTIONS

GETTING DISTRACTED

FOCUS

BRINGING YOUR ATTENTION BACK TO YOUR BREATHING

NOTICING THAT YOU'RE DISTRACTED AND BRINGING YOUR MIND BACK TO WHAT YOU WANT TO FOCUS ON, IS A KEY MENTAL MUSCLE TO BUILD.

FOCUS

FOCUS

FLOWER!!

AFTER EACH GO, ASK YOURSELF:

★ **How long did I sit still for?**

_____

★ **What did I notice?**

_____

_____

_____

_____

_____

_____

★ **When my mind drifted, how did I bring it back to the activity?**

_____

_____

_____

_____

_____

_____

★ **How did I feel?**

_____

_____

_____

_____

_____

_____

★ **What thoughts and ideas did I have?**

_____

_____

_____

_____

_____

_____

★ **Who do I want to talk to about this experience?**

_____

_____

★ **How was the overall experience?** ☺ 😐 ☹

As you practise this activity, you might notice that you can do it for longer each time. Maybe your first effort is 10 seconds, then your second effort is 15 seconds. Over time, you might make it to 5 minutes. But whether you get to that or not, the power of the activity is more in trying to take time away from distractions.

You could try this activity for 5 minutes every day, or just 5 minutes every week. See what feels right for you. Each time you try it, no matter how long you manage to do it for, give yourself a pat on the back. You've just done something that people all around the world avoid doing every day . . .

BEING STILL
AND THINKING!

AND AS YOU DO IT MORE AND MORE, YOU WILL GET TO KNOW YOURSELF BETTER AND BRING YOUR DREAMS UP TO THE SURFACE. ONCE YOU KNOW WHAT YOUR DREAMS ARE, YOU CAN START WORKING TOWARDS MAKING THEM COME TRUE. AND THAT'S WHAT I'M GOING TO HELP YOU DO IN THE REST OF THIS BOOK.

HAVE ANY OF YOUR DREAMS COME TO THE SURFACE?
HAVE A GO AT WRITING THEM DOWN HERE!

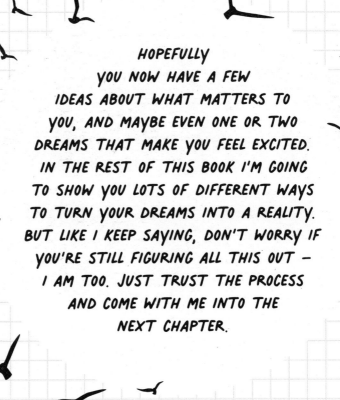

HOPEFULLY
YOU NOW HAVE A FEW
IDEAS ABOUT WHAT MATTERS TO
YOU, AND MAYBE EVEN ONE OR TWO
DREAMS THAT MAKE YOU FEEL EXCITED.
IN THE REST OF THIS BOOK I'M GOING
TO SHOW YOU LOTS OF DIFFERENT WAYS
TO TURN YOUR DREAMS INTO A REALITY.
BUT LIKE I KEEP SAYING, DON'T WORRY IF
YOU'RE STILL FIGURING ALL THIS OUT –
I AM TOO. JUST TRUST THE PROCESS
AND COME WITH ME INTO THE
NEXT CHAPTER.

MINDSET MATTERS

NOW THAT WE'VE EXPLORED YOUR HOPES AND DREAMS, IT'S TIME TO TALK ABOUT HOW TO MAKE THEM COME TRUE!

This is where **MINDSET** really matters. It's probably the single most important thing that will affect your life and your happiness. Put simply, your mindset is your attitude – it influences the way you see yourself (like who you are, what you're capable of and what you deserve) and the world (how it works, what to expect and what's possible). It powers your thoughts, feelings and behaviour.

Rather than thinking of 'good' and 'bad' mindsets, I want you to think of **'useful'** and **'less-useful'** mindsets. A useful mindset is one that helps you move towards your goals, be the person you want to be and make the most of your potential. A less-useful mindset does the opposite. But the great news is that you can learn to create the mindset you want to have!

When you read the word **'IMPOSSIBLE'** can you do anything else with those letters other than spell out the word impossible?

If you open your mind, can you see **'I'M POSSIBLE'** in there too?

Do you ever find yourself in a situation that feels uncomfortable or stressful? Don't get me wrong, this happens to us all, but sometimes choosing a different mindset can change your experience. There's a saying that goes

'WHEN YOU CHANGE THE WAY YOU LOOK AT THINGS,
THE THINGS YOU LOOK AT CHANGE'.

I want to show you what I mean. When I was younger, I had real problems learning how to swim. My technique was ok – I knew how to do front crawl and backstroke and all that – but I really didn't want to swim in the deep end of the pool, where my feet wouldn't touch the ground. I always wanted to swim in the shallow end of the pool because I didn't think my swimming was good enough. Over time, my swimming teachers helped me understand that my swimming *was* strong enough for the deep end, and that if I got stuck I could swim back to the safer, shallower areas. I just had to try it!

I had to change my mindset from **'my swimming isn't good enough'** to **'I trust that I can get better'**, in order to get past that challenge. It could be the same for you.

The first mindset in my swimming example
is what I call a

But I managed to change my way of thinking to a

A **LIMITED MINDSET** places limits on what you can achieve in life. It's the idea that there is only one way to do something, and it's not okay if things don't go your way. In this mindset you won't try to achieve your dreams, because the journey seems too hard.

A **LIMITLESS MINDSET** is the idea that there are endless opportunities in life. It's believing that great things can be accomplished through courage, persistence and teamwork. This type of thinking allows you to do things when others say they are impossible. It is a major step towards becoming the champion that you truly are.

TAKE A LOOK AT HOW PEOPLE WHO HAVE A LIMITLESS MINDSET MIGHT THINK, COMPARED TO PEOPLE IN A LIMITED MINDSET.

Core Belief
I am the way I am, and I can't change that.

Effort
There's no point in trying, I'll never get better. I'm embarrass to put in effort, beca people will think that I'm not clever or talented.

Mistakes
I blame others when mistakes happen. I focus on the fact that life is unfair.

LIMITED MINDSET

Other People's Achievements
Something to be jealous of.

Focus
I focus on the things I can't control.

Setbacks
Setbacks are embarrassing – it's best not to try.

My Success
The way to measure my success is by beating everyone else, and trying to be the person that others expect me to be.

Core Belief
Life is full of opportunities for me to go after.

Effort
Putting in effort is essential to progress and trying new things is fun!

Mistakes
I accept that mistakes happen and think about what I can do better next time. Go again!

LIMITLESS MINDSET

Other People's Achievements
Something I can take inspiration from.

Focus
I focus only on the things I can control.

My Success
The way to measure my success is by trying my best and being true to myself.

Setbacks
Setbacks are part of the journey to success – it shows that I tried!

WHICH MINDSET DO YOU THINK YOU HAVE? ON THE LINE BELOW, MARK WHERE YOU THINK YOU SPEND MOST OF YOUR TIME.

LIMITED   **LIMITLESS**

If you think you spend more time in a **Limited Mindset**, try not to be so hard on yourself. I bet you're not in it all the time. If you had to find an example of when you were in a **Limitless Mindset**, what would you choose? (Here's a hint – the fact you're even reading this book proves you're trying to have more of a **Limitless Mindset!**)

If you're anything like me, you've probably got a mixture of **Limitless Mindset** and **Limited Mindset**. We're not robots and lots of things influence our mindset every day (like if we're hungry or tired!) but like I said, we can try to change our mindset.

Have a go at writing down some thoughts you might have had whilst in a **Limited Mindset** – this could be from a time when you were trying a new sport, doing homework, or talking to friends. How can you change your **Limited Mindset** into a **Limitless** one?

Marcus's limited mindset: *SWIMMING IS NOT MY THING.*
Marcus's limitless mindset: *I CAN GET BETTER AT SWIMMING.*

★ My LIMITED mindset thinks

_____

I can turn this into a LIMITLESS mindset by thinking:

_____

★ My LIMITED mindset thinks

_____

I can turn this into a LIMITLESS mindset by thinking:

_____

★ My LIMITED mindset thinks

_____

I can turn this into a LIMITLESS mindset by thinking:

_____

★ My LIMITED mindset thinks

_____

I can turn this into a LIMITLESS mindset by thinking:

_____

★ My LIMITED mindset thinks

_____

I can turn this into a LIMITLESS mindset by thinking:

_____

When you've finished, read back through them and ask
yourself:

★ Which of your answers would you choose if you had full
control of your thoughts?

★ Which of your answers would bring more positive
things into your life?

★ Which of your answers bring you closer to becoming
the champion you want to be?

IT DOESN'T MATTER
WHERE YOU'RE STARTING
FROM ON YOUR JOURNEY TO A
LIMITLESS MINDSET. IT'S JUST
GREAT TO HAVE YOU WITH ME ON THIS
ADVENTURE. CREATING A LIMITLESS
MINDSET IS A CHOICE AND A SKILL.
IT IS SOMETHING THAT WE CAN
WORK ON BY BUILDING MORE
MENTAL MUSCLE!

MENTAL MUSCLE ACTIVITY

Every day is an opportunity to build the **MENTAL MUSCLE** needed to step into a **Limitless Mindset**, so I want you to get into the habit of doing something positive for your mind every day! By following this weekly plan, you will build up the mental ingredients of a **Limitless Mindset**.

MONDAY

On three separate post-it notes, write down three things you are good at. Stick them to your mirror, your wall, or your door — somewhere where you'll see them every day. Make sure to read them each morning, and then decide how you could use those strengths in the day ahead. For example, is your strength that you're funny? If so, you could try making people laugh at lunchtime!

TUESDAY

Imagine you have a pocket-sized version of someone who is totally on your side. Imagine what they'd say to encourage you through your day. It could even be me; literally a singing and dancing mini-Marcus in your pocket rooting for you!

WEDNESDAY

At the end of the day, write down three things you did well that day. It could be things like 'I remembered to take the right kit into school', or 'I helped my parents' or even something as simple as 'I smiled at someone who looked like they were having a tough day'. There is nothing too big or too small for this list, and trying to do the right thing counts as well!

THURSDAY

As the week goes on, do you find yourself getting tired, frustrated or impatient? If so, have a go at shaking it out — literally shake your arms, legs and head, and imagine shaking out the feeling. You might feel silly doing it but trust me, it works a treat. Sometimes I do a big pretend yawn to let go of any stress I'm holding in my jaw — you can try that too!

FRIDAY

Do something that scares you today. Don't get me wrong, don't get into trouble or danger, but take a little risk, be with those tricky thoughts and feelings that naturally pop up when we step out of our comfort zone. We often wait to feel confident before we try something, but the best way to build your confidence is to take action. This could be something like asking for help when you were confused in class, rather than being quiet and hoping for the best. Or joining a sports team even though your mind is telling you 'I'm not good enough'. In a **Limitless Mindset** we still have worries and doubts, we just don't listen to them!

SATURDAY

Choose someone who you care about. It could be someone who believes in you or a friend you have a good laugh with. Let them know what you appreciate about them. Notice how they react and how that makes you feel.

SUNDAY

CHILL OUT!

WHEN YOU GET TO THE END OF THE WEEK GIVE YOURSELF A BIG PAT ON THE BACK!

Ready for a new week? Now you can do it again, mix it up and have a go at making your own **MENTAL MUSCLE** planner. Don't worry if you miss a day or a even a week, life gets in the way sometimes. You can talk to a friend or family member for suggestions and just try to get back on track the next day. Most importantly, don't forget to have fun with this! Every day is an opportunity to build your mental muscle by thinking about and choosing a **Limitless Mindset.**

You might notice a few of those activities involve writing things down. You don't have to show anyone your scribbles but writing things down can really help develop your mindset. When we write things down, it helps us hear ourselves and make sense of our thoughts and feelings. From there it's easier to understand how we really feel or what action we need to take.

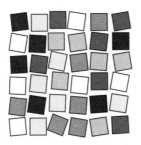

MY BRAIN BEFORE WRITING STUFF DOWN

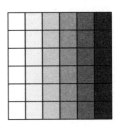

MY BRAIN AFTER WRITING STUFF DOWN

MASTERING YOUR MOMENTUM

Have you ever thought about how many choices you make every day? From what you can have for breakfast, to what you do after school, to what you should watch on TV? Some of the choices you make move you towards your dreams and goals. I call this **BUILDING MOMENTUM.**

To be the best footballer I can be, I do the following things to BUILD MOMENTUM:

- ★ Ask my coach for feedback and really listen to what they say.
- ★ Watch my games back to analyse my performance and work out what I can do better next time.
- ★ Have a clear aim for every training session.

When life is good, it's quite easy to build momentum. But life isn't always that easy. Do you ever find yourself in difficult situations where you're not sure what to do? Maybe negative thoughts take over your mind, making you feel confused, sad or angry?

I'M NOT GOOD ENOUGH

THIS WILL NEVER WORK

LIFE SUCKS

We can easily get caught up with those difficult thoughts and feelings, and this can lead us to make choices that take us away from the person we want to be and the things we want to achieve. I call these thoughts **SLOWING MOMENTUM**.

If I want to be the best footballer I can be, I need to be mindful of things that can SLOW MY MOMENTUM, like:

★ Staying up late playing computer games – it's fun in the moment, but I regret it when I wake up tired and can't train as hard.

★ Getting stuck thinking about one or two mistakes I made in a game, and ignoring all the effort I put in.

★ Thinking about football all the time – I love the sport, but it's important to switch off from time to time and just be me. If I don't do this, I get a bit burnt out.

I want you to become more aware of how you **BUILD MOMENTUM** and **SLOW MOMENTUM**. Knowing how to do this is a big step towards being the very best version of you that you can be.

COMPLETE THE FOLLOWING SENTENCES, AND TRY TO BE AS CLEAR AND SPECIFIC AS POSSIBLE WITH WHAT YOU WRITE DOWN.

My current dream is

_____

_____

_____

To BUILD MOMENTUM towards this dream I can

1. _____

_____

2. _____

_____

3. _____

_____

Thoughts and actions I want to watch out for which might SLOW MOMENTUM are

1. _____

_____

_____

2. _____

_____

_____

3. _____

_____

_____

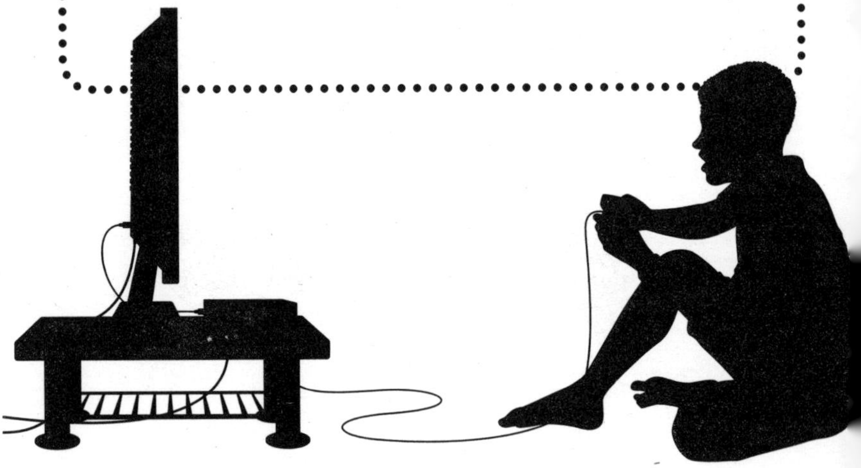

You might be thinking 'but why would I ever deliberately slow my momentum?' Hear me out. Young people make about 3,500 choices every day.

WHAT SHALL I HAVE FOR BREAKFAST?

WHAT SHALL I WEAR TODAY?

WHAT BOOK SHALL I READ?

Each of these choices comes from a choice point – literally a point where you could go one way or another. Sometimes we move through choice points without realising it, or we make choices that aren't that helpful.

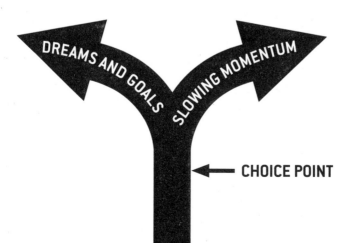

DREAMS AND GOALS

SLOWING MOMENTUM

← **CHOICE POINT**

Sometimes tricky thoughts pop up from the **Limited Mindset** that take us in the wrong direction.

This is why we need **MENTAL MUSCLE** – to unhook from difficult thoughts and feelings and choose to **BUILD MOMENTUM** instead.

YOU CAN'T ALWAYS CONTROL YOUR THOUGHTS
BUT YOU CAN
LEARN TO CHOOSE
HOW YOU RESPOND TO THEM.

It's a bit like football — I can't control the passes that come my way, but I can choose how I respond. It's the difference between thinking:

I CAN'T DO IT SO I SHOULD STOP TRYING.

AND

I HAVEN'T BEEN ABLE TO DO IT YET SO I WILL TRY AGAIN!

Later in this journey I'll share different ways to let go of tricky thoughts, but for now it's great simply to think about how how you can **BUILD MOMENTUM** towards achieving your dreams. Eventually you will be able to see how often you can coach yourself into making the right choice.

FUEL YOUR
ADVENTURES

WRITE DOWN ALL OF THE PEOPLE WHO ARE ON YOUR *TEAM* - EVERYONE WHO SUPPORTS YOU ON YOUR LIFE'S JOURNEY. YOU COULD EVEN HAVE A GO AT DRAWING THEM!

When you're finished, take a look at your list. Some people have a long list of names, while others have a shorter one. At the top of my list are my mum, my siblings, my best friend Jamie and my fiancée Lucia. It is different for everyone, and I don't want you to get too hung up on how many people are on your list.

THE MOST IMPORTANT THING IS THAT YOUR NAME APPEARS ON THAT LIST TOO. DID YOU WRITE YOUR NAME DOWN? IF NOT, GO AND ADD IT RIGHT NOW!

When I play football, there are thousands, if not millions of people, cheering me on to do my best. That support means a lot, but it's really important that I am cheering myself on too.

IN LIFE, THERE WILL BE TIMES WHERE YOU WILL HAVE TO BE YOUR BIGGEST SUPPORTER! It starts with taking care of the basics, and I want to show you why these are central to you being the champion that you really are.

FIRST UP: SLEEP

I want you to trust me when I say that sleep is really important. When I was younger I never wanted to go to bed early (I used to be a real pain to my mum!) but now I'm older, I realise that sleep is important for everything that follows in my day. During a football season I have to sleep at least eight hours at night, and then on top of that I have to sleep for about 90 minutes when I get home after football training so my body has the time it needs to rest and recover. When I sleep, my brain also takes in everything I learnt on the pitch that day so that I can be better tomorrow.

Here are some fun facts about sleep:

★ **A giraffe only needs 2 hours of sleep per day.**

★ **A bat needs 20 hours.**

★ **You will spend around a THIRD of your life asleep.**

★ **Sleep is one of the most powerful things you can do to take care of your mind and body.**

★ **Humans are the only species on the planet to delay sleep – we put it off to watch TV, see friends and play computer games. Every time we do this, we're denting our MENTAL MUSCLE.**

SLEEP IS SO IMPORTANT.

It can boost:

★ What you get done in a day.

★ Positivity – our brains are up to 60% more positive when we've had a good sleep.

★ How well your body fights off illness.

★ Fitness and health – the body often repairs itself when you're asleep (a bit like when you put a smartphone on charge!).

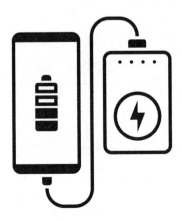

MENTAL MUSCLE ACTIVITY

TIME TO FIND OUT WHETHER YOU ARE ALL RIGHT AT NIGHT! CIRCLE YOUR ANSWERS TO THE BELOW QUESTIONS:

How many nights a week do you sleep for 10–12 hours? (That's roughly how much you should be getting per night!)
a) None
b) 3–4
c) 6–7

How often do you wake up feeling fresh and ready to take on the day?
a) Never – I want to hit snooze and get back under the duvet.
b) 3–4
c) 6–7 – can't hold me back!

Roughly how long does it take you to fall asleep?
a) Ages
b) A little while
c) Who knows, I'm out like a light!

NOW IT'S TIME TO FIND OUT YOUR SCORE. HERE'S HOW TO WORK IT OUT:

a's = 1 point   b's = 3 points   c's = 6 points

If you scored 8 or fewer = It's amazing that you're achieving what you are with so little sleep. Imagine what might be possible if you slept more! Have a read of my helpful tricks on the next page and make one or two small changes to help your mind and body out.

If you scored 9–14 = You're on the right track to sleeping like a champion, but your mind and body will thank you for making a few small changes in the sleep zone. Choose 1–2 helpful hints on the next page to boost yourself.

If you scored 15+ = You're sleeping like a champion. Keep it up.

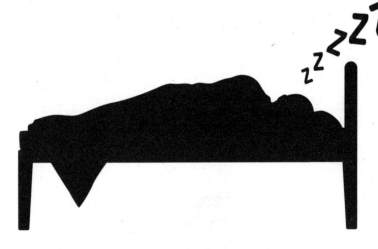

*HERE ARE MY HELPFUL HINTS TO HELP YOU WORK
TOWARDS BECOMING A CHAMPION SLEEPER:*

★ Get lots of it (10–12 hours if you can!)

★ Try to go to bed and wake up at roughly the same time
each day.

★ Make a bedtime routine where you start winding down
an hour before sleep time. This could involve turning off
bright lights, no screens, reading a book or thinking about
what went well in your day – as you do this something
called MELATONIN will be released in your body which will
help you fall asleep.

★ Have a hot bath or shower if you can – after this your body
cools down which will help you fall asleep.

★ When you're in bed, just chill. Sleep is a natural process,
don't force it!

★ Bad dreams? Write a story about your bad dream and give
it a fun ending.

I always try to go to my bedroom at the same time every night, with a big glass of water. I make sure my bed is as clean and comfortable as possible, and then I'll put on some chilled out music that I really like. I slowly drink my water and think back through my day. When I'm ready to go to sleep I try to focus on my breathing – I like to imagine there is a feather on my nose, and when I breathe in and breathe out, I watch how the feather moves. I want to make my breaths slow so the feather never falls off.

APPARENTLY, TWO THIRDS OF ADULTS DON'T GET ENOUGH SLEEP, SO HERE'S YOUR CHANCE TO SHOW THEM HOW IT'S DONE!

YOU KNOW HOW THEY
SAY YOU SHOULD

COUNT
SHEEP

WHEN YOU CAN'T SLEEP?
THAT'S TO GIVE YOUR
MIND SOMETHING TO
FOCUS ON WHILE THE
NATURAL PROCESS OF
SLEEP TAKES OVER!

NEXT UP: MOVE YOUR BODY

You probably already know that it's good to move your body, but did you know that over half of the UK's young people don't get enough exercise? So, how active are you? Write down as many examples as you'd like of how you keep active – this could be things from playing sport, to walking, to helping out around the house.

If you're already pretty active, great work! If you're not, don't worry – we can work on it together. You don't have to be a top footballer, runner or gymnast to get active. Any kind of movement is good.

And being active is as good for your brain as it is for your body. *JUST 10 MINUTES OF MOVING YOUR BODY MAKES YOUR BRAIN STRONGER.* You'll be able to think more clearly after and will feel good too.

Here are a few simple ideas to help you get more active:

★ When you get dressed for school, stand in front of the mirror, do 5 star jumps and have a little chat with yourself. Tell yourself how you're going to try to move your body today.

★ When you're out and about, take the stairs two at a time if you can.

★ If you get the bus, get off one stop earlier and walk to your destination.

★ Find a sport that you love – it doesn't matter what it is, as long as you enjoy it.

★ Make a pact with a friend to be active every day of the week.

★ Ask yourself: have you ever regretted being active? If you have, think about why that is, and what you can do to fix it for next time.

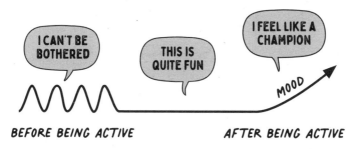

BEFORE BEING ACTIVE   **AFTER BEING ACTIVE**

MENTAL MUSCLE ACTIVITY

I've had lots of amazing coaches who help me enjoy playing football. I want you to imagine you have your very own coach who is going to help you enjoy being active every day. Draw your coach below and fill in the speech bubbles for the positive, kind and encouraging things they would say to you before, during and after exercising.

MENTAL MUSCLE ACTIVITY

Think about one thing that you do that's important to you or really good for you. For example, taking care of your pet, being kind to others, going to bed a bit earlier. Now write a thank you card to yourself! Thank yourself for doing that one thing. You could write about what it is, why you do it and how it helps you to be the champion you are.

You don't need to make massive
changes to become a champion
sleeper and get more active.
Small changes will add up to big
results. So make one small promise
to yourself that you can keep each
day, and over time those
small actions will add up
to big change.

BUILD YOUR TEAM

WHEN I LOOK BACK AT ALL OF THE THINGS THAT I'VE ACHIEVED IN MY LIFE SO FAR, I IMMEDIATELY SEE IN MY MIND ALL OF THE PEOPLE WHO HAVE HELPED ME ALONG THE WAY.

There was Greg, who owned the local shop down my street and looked out for me and my family. There's my mate Jamie, who helped me when I was recovering from my football injuries. There are my siblings, who help me try to do better in everything I do. And of course, there is my mum, Melanie, who is my inspiration for everything.

Each of them have given me something different — from support and encouragement, to lifts to football training … and even the occasional telling off when I needed it! They all believed in me, and that belief helped me find the courage to follow my dreams. I know how important it is to have a strong group of people around me, and I want to talk to you about how to build your team so that you can feel supported on your journey too.

Being in a team is part of being human. Back in the days of cavemen and cavewomen, humans were able to survive in a dangerous world because they were able to work together. They weren't faster, stronger or bigger than the animals at the time, but they were much better at working together and supporting each other.

HUMANS NEED SUPPORT FROM OTHER PEOPLE FROM THE DAY THEY'RE BORN.

Have you spent much time around babies? If so, you've probably noticed that they can't do much! Human babies are born with a gap in their skull, their necks are so weak that they can't hold their own head up straight and their fingers are tiny – it will take years before they're ready to be independent! When I was a baby, *IT TOOK ME ABOUT 10 MONTHS TO WALK!*

It's really different in the animal kingdom. A newborn baby rabbit is born blind and without fur, but within 3 weeks it will be ready to leave the nest and live on its own. A baby lizard is expected to fend for itself after just two days! On average, a baby giraffe can walk after 30 minutes!

But us humans, we're wired to be close to other people. Throughout your life you'll need people around you who will love and support you for who you are. People who really see you, listen to you, value you and who will make you feel stronger, so that you can be the best version of you that you can possibly be.

DID YOU KNOW THAT WHEN YOU SPEND TIME WITH PEOPLE YOU CARE ABOUT YOUR HEART RATES CAN START BEATING IN SYNCH — YOUR HEARTS CAN LITERALLY MATCH EACH OTHER!

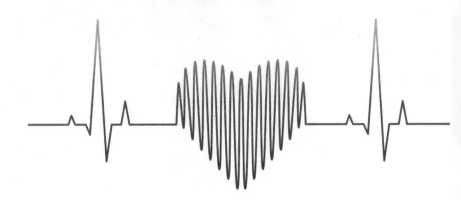

So, who's in your team?

MENTAL MUSCLE ACTIVITY

WRITE DOWN THE NAMES OF UP TO 5 PEOPLE WHO ARE IN YOUR TEAM. This could be anyone you feel able to be yourself around, who cares for you or who you look up to — from friends, to family, to teachers, to people in your community.

1. _____

2. _____

3. _____

4. _____

5. _____

When you've finished, read back through them and ask yourself:

★ **What are they good at?**

★ **How does being around them make you feel?**

★ **What do you appreciate about them?**

★ **When was the last time you said thank you for their support?**

If your answer to the last question was **'not recently'**, then now is the time! I want you to let them know that you appreciate them and are grateful for their support in the next 5 days. It's so important to look after your team. All sorts of great things can happen when you do this.

Things like:

★ They feel appreciated.

★ You feel clearer about what you're grateful for.

★ They understand the important role they play in your life.

★ You feel more motivated because of the strength of your team.

★ They may want to support you even more.

★ You never know what someone is going through – being kind might make all the difference.

★ It might inspire them to support others too.

DID YOU KNOW YOU HAVE A SUPERPOWER?

Have you ever wondered why pea and Brussels sprout ice-cream doesn't exist? If it did, would you eat it?

IF YOU'RE THINKING 'EUGH!' ME TOO!

Perhaps the reason it doesn't exist is because we can imagine what it would taste like.

Our ability to imagine things is a real superpower. When you imagine yourself doing something you wake up a certain part of your brain, and the exact same part of the brain is activated when you physically do it! Before football games I always try to imagine myself playing well, helping my teammates out and scoring goals, because imagining it is the first step in actually achieving those things.

I want to show you what I mean. **Close your eyes and imagine the letter A.** When you do that, you get the same part of your brain working as when you are actually looking at the letter A.

Are you left handed or right handed? I want you to imagine you are writing your name with the hand you normally write with. Chances are, it will take you a similar amount of time to imagine doing it as when you actually write it out.

Now imagine writing your name with your other hand. Did it take you longer to imagine it? That's because the parts of your brain you use to do that are not as strong, because you don't practise actually writing with that hand!

MENTAL MUSCLE ACTIVITY

If you could have anyone in your team, who would you choose? It could be a sportsperson, an actor, a scientist, a campaigner, a character in a book or a film – you can choose literally anyone who inspires you!

Using your imagination superpower, think of someone who you've never met who you'd like to add to your team. Draw a picture of them below and think about what they would say to you to support you on your journey.

The person I would like to add to my support team is

_____

I am choosing them because

_____

I would like to ask them

_____

I imagine they would tell me

_____

Now you've spent some time thinking about who's in your team and what you appreciate about them, it's time to think about what makes your team special. Here's an activity to help you find out:

1. **In the 3 circles on the next page, write your name in one and the name of two friends in the other ones.**

2. **In your circle, write down something that you are good at.**

3. **Repeat this for your friends – in their circles, write down something they are good at.**

4. **Now try to think about something you have in common with each of your friends. It could be a band you like, or something that you both care about. Write that bit in the parts which overlap.**

5. **Now write something that connects all 3 of you in the middle. Don't take the easy option here, like 'we all go to the same school'. Challenge yourself to find something that is special to the three of you.**

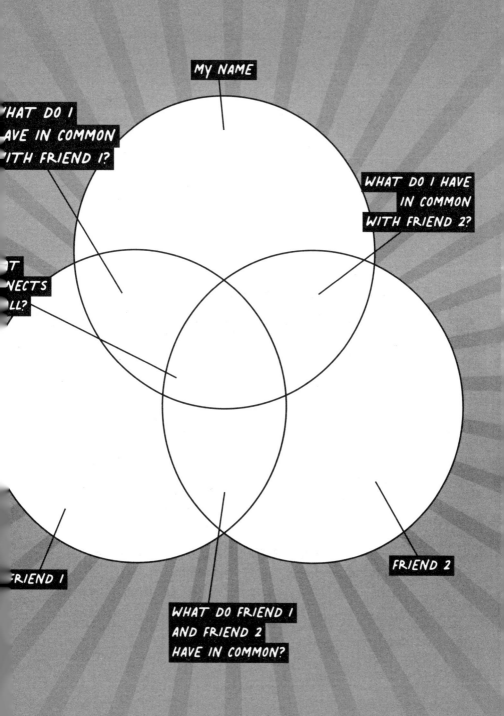

Thinking about what connects you to your teammates will help strengthen the bonds between you all. It's also a great way to celebrate our differences – *YOU WOULDN'T WANT A BAND WITH ONLY GUITAR PLAYERS, OR A FOOTBALL TEAM WITH ONLY DEFENDERS!*

Great teams have great people in them, but it's more than just collecting the 11 best players in the world and asking them to figure it out. The best teams bring together great people, but they also make sure there's loads of joined up thinking between them. A good centre-back partnership has two players whose strengths and weaknesses complement each other. If one player likes to tackle early, then the other player is good at reading space and figuring out when those tackles need to be made. Good teams and good partnerships come about when your skills match, but also when you communicate and respect each other. We understand that it isn't going to be perfect every time, but as long as we all try our best and want the same thing, it will come good in the end.

I want to introduce you to something called **Triple H** (not the wrestler!). This is something we do in our football team to help people get to know each other, and it helps me to feel a lot closer to my teammates.

All you have to do is get together with one or two friends and talk about:

★ **A HERO** – someone you look up to and why.

★ **A HARDSHIP** – a tough experience you had, how you felt at the time and maybe what you learnt from it too.

★ **A HIGHLIGHT** – something that made you happy or you're proud of.

I find that sharing my **Triple H** makes me feel a lot closer to my team, and listening to their answers helps me understand them more too.

TO HELP YOU PREPARE, HAVE A GO AT
WRITING DOWN YOUR TRIPLE H:

★ MY HERO:

_____

_____

_____

★ MY HARDSHIP:

_____

_____

_____

_____

★ MY HIGHLIGHT:

_____

_____

_____

_____

AFTER YOU'VE DONE TRIPLE H WITH YOUR TEAM, HAVE A GO AT ANSWERING THESE QUESTIONS:

1. Who did you try Triple H with?

   _____

   _____

2. How did you feel before doing it?

   _____

   _____

3. What did you learn about your team?

   _____

   _____

4. How did you feel after trying the activity?

   _____

   _____

   _____

5. Did you feel closer to each other or more able to trust them?

   _____

   _____

When I think about the best teams I've been in, we've had a real laugh together and we always try to support each other as best we can. But even in the best teams, there are going to be some times when things get tough, and it's actually getting through those tough times that can make us feel closer. Have a think about the following questions:

WHEN IS THE LAST TIME YOU TOLD SOMEONE THE TRUTH ABOUT HOW YOU FEEL?

WHEN IS THE LAST TIME SOMEONE CHALLENGED YOU TO DO SOMETHING BETTER?

Imagine you and your friend want to write a book. You agree the title and what it's going to be about, and then they promise to write the first chapter, while you write the second.

When you get together, they haven't done their bit. You feel upset and frustrated.

Now you have a choice:
OPTION 1: Pretend it doesn't matter and make a joke of it.
OPTION 2: Be honest with them in a positive way.

OPTION 1 probably feels more comfortable in the moment, but how do you feel after? When I choose that path, I know that what I've really done is kick the problem further down the line. But the thing about kicking problems further down the line is you have to deal with them eventually. And the more you kick them down the line, the bigger they get, because they collect other problems with it.

This is why I try my best to do **OPTION 2**. It might be uncomfortable in the moment, but I promise it will lead to a better place. Being honest can help us understand what is important to each other and become more aware of the impact we have on others. Caring about our impact on others and doing something about it brings us closer.

Here's a simple trick I use when I have to be honest with someone in my team. It spells out the word **'BEING'**.

BE = BEHAVIOUR

e.g. We agreed you would write chapter 1 and you haven't done it.

I = IMPACT

This makes me feel bad because we had a deal and now we're behind with our plan.

N = NEEDS

I need to understand what stopped you doing it and how we get over that.

G = GOALS

Let's set a new goal to finish chapter 1 by next week.

Giving out tough love is one part of being in a winning team, and so is taking it! No one is perfect and if you're challenging yourself to follow your dreams, the chances are you'll make some mistakes.

There's a saying that goes

YOU HAVE TO CRACK A FEW EGGS TO MAKE AN OMELETTE.

It means if you want to achieve something, sometimes you have to make some mistakes.

If you find yourself in a **LIMITED mindset**, you might want to make excuses, blame others or be too hard on yourself. Tough love is about stepping into a **LIMITLESS mindset** — there's nothing we can't talk about together as we work towards our dreams. That said, there's a skill to having these conversations in a positive way so that you can move forward together.

It's hard to hear that your actions have hurt someone, especially someone who's in your team, but it's important that you listen to each other and work together to move forward from any setbacks. In the previous exercise we worked on how you can positively let other people know when they've hurt you, but now I want to show you a trick for how you can move forward when your positions are reversed. I like to keep things simple, and this one spells out the word **LAST**.

L = **Listen to what they are saying.**

A = **Ask questions to check you have understood it.**

S = **Solution – suggest ways you can fix the situation.**

T = **Thank you – say thank you to them for being honest with you.**

I HOPE THESE LITTLE TRICKS HELP. THE KEY IS TO PRACTISE THEM AND OVER TIME IT WILL START TO FEEL REALLY NATURAL.

Before we finish this chapter, here are my top tips for getting the best out of your friendships in life:

★ Be yourself. The right people will like you for who you are.

★ Think about the kind of friend you want to be.

★ Be interested in your friends. Ask them questions and really listen to what they say. Remember little things like their birthday.

★ Celebrate your friends' achievements.

★ If they seem quiet or angry, ask them how you can help.

★ Tell them what you really think and feel about important things in your life.

★ If you find yourself getting grumpy with someone, ask yourself 'what do I like about this person?' Sometimes we just need to be reminded.

★ If you get something wrong, say sorry. I haven't always liked saying sorry but if I follow four simple steps, it seems to go quite well:

- **STEP ONE:**
  You know when I did / said . . .

- **STEP TWO:**
  What I did was wrong

- **STEP THREE:**
  I'm sorry I hurt you

- **STEP FOUR:**
  How can I make it up to you?

REMEMBER, YOU
CAN COME BACK TO THE
ACTIVITIES IN THIS CHAPTER
ANY TIME. WHETHER YOU DREAM
OF PLAYING FOOTBALL, ACTING ON
THE BIG STAGE OR SIMPLY HAVING
FUN DAY TO DAY, HAVING PEOPLE
AROUND YOU TO SHARE THE
JOURNEY WITH IS WHAT
IT'S ALL ABOUT.

SUCCESS AND SETBACKS

You've already done so much great work so far. You've started to think about your dreams, you're training your **LIMITLESS MINDSET**, fuelling yourself right through sleep and exercise, and you're building your team.

But despite all this great champion behaviour, you're still going to meet some bumps on your journey. It's all part of the process.

IT'S RARE FOR A FOOTBALL TEAM TO PLAY THE PERFECT GAME, AND IT'S RARER STILL FOR A TEAM TO PLAY PERFECTLY ACROSS A SEASON.

Sir Alex Ferguson is regarded as one of the greatest football managers of all time. He led Manchester United to many Premier League titles and triumphs. He won a lot of games, but he also lost a fair few as well.

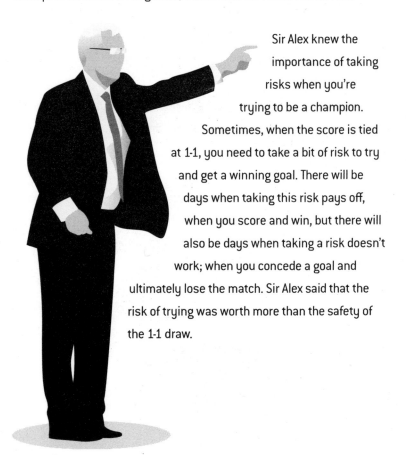

Sir Alex knew the importance of taking risks when you're trying to be a champion. Sometimes, when the score is tied at 1-1, you need to take a bit of risk to try and get a winning goal. There will be days when taking this risk pays off, when you score and win, but there will also be days when taking a risk doesn't work; when you concede a goal and ultimately lose the match. Sir Alex said that the risk of trying was worth more than the safety of the 1-1 draw.

People often think of **success** and **setbacks** as opposites, but that's not quite right. In fact, setbacks are simply a stepping stone on the *way* to success.

WE THINK OF
FAILURE AND SUCCESS AS
OPPOSITES
WHEN IN REALITY FAILURE
IS PART OF SUCCESS.

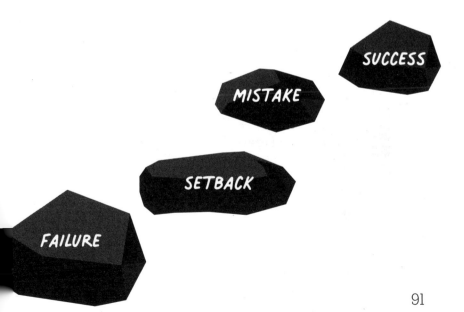

I've had a few setbacks in my life so far: I've played in a Europa League Final and won, but I also played in a Europa League Final and lost. I've won the FA Cup, but I've also lost in an FA Cup Final. And then there's the penalty I missed for England in the final of the UEFA European Championship — that will stay with me forever. I hope that I'll have more setbacks and failures in my future, because that will mean I'm trying new things and pushing myself to achieve my dreams.

SETBACKS MAKE YOU
BETTER.

They will help you to learn and move you one step closer to finding the answer. *BUT IT'S IMPORTANT TO REMEMBER THAT A SETBACK DOESN'T DEFINE YOU. IT'S WHAT YOU DO NEXT THAT MATTERS.*

MENTAL MUSCLE ACTIVITY

ARE THERE ANY TIMES WHEN YOU'VE FELT LIKE YOU'VE HAD A SETBACK? WRITE A COUPLE OF EXAMPLES BELOW.

1. _____
_____
_____
_____

2. _____
_____
_____
_____

3. _____
_____
_____
_____

How did it make you feel to do that activity? When I think about the times things didn't go how I wanted them to, it can make me feel sad. I wish I could go back and change those moments; I wish I could redo that penalty for England and that things would be different. But then I remind myself that everyone has setbacks from time to time.

THE ONLY REAL WAY TO FAIL IS TO GIVE UP ON TRYING.

I've said this before, but one of my coaches told me that

FOOTBALL IS A GAME OF MISTAKES.

If no one made a mistake playing football, then every game would finish 0-0 and everything would be boring. Most goals happen because someone, somewhere, made a mistake when defending, and some of the greatest goals ever scored have come about from someone, somewhere, trying something they probably shouldn't have.

Can you think of any ways that the setbacks you wrote on the previous page made you stronger? What did you learn from them?

To make the most of your setbacks, we need to be in the **LIMITLESS MINDSET:**

	LIMITED MINDSET	LIMITLESS MINDSET
Beliefs about Setbacks	It's not a good thing. It means I'm not good enough.	It's a natural part of trying new things. I'm learning.
The Goal	Avoid failing.	Learn quickly.
Beliefs about Champions	Champions don't fail.	Champions fail regularly, learn from their setbacks and share that learning to help others to succeed, too.

Being in a **LIMITLESS MINDSET** is a choice and a skill. Like all skills, the more you work at it, the easier it becomes.

I need to be honest with you though, when it comes to setbacks and failure, stepping into a **Limitless Mindset** can be really tricky. To explain what I mean, we need to get in a time machine and travel back to the Stone Age.

If you had been born 300,000 years ago, you would have been a caveman or cavewoman. You might have been called Eev, Dia, Unk and Ork!

Life was pretty dangerous back then. You'd need to be on the lookout for poisonous plants, cavepeople from rival tribes and even tigers trying to eat you! With all of this danger around, the main goal was to stay alive and not get eaten. To help them do this, cavepeople developed brains that were very good at:

✦ **Recognising fear**

✦ **Imagining the worst case scenario**

✦ **Looking out for danger**

Imagine two cavepeople called Alex and Tunde. Alex is relaxed, happy and confident. Tunde worries about everything and is not very confident. They're both out looking for berries. Suddenly, they hear a rustling in the bushes. Alex, being happy and relaxed, assumes it's a friend and moves towards the rustling to say hello. Tunde, being unsure of everything, decides it's an animal getting ready to attack.

If it is a predator, Alex is more likely to be eaten and Tunde is more likely to survive. If it's a friend, then no harm done and Tunde can come out to play when they're confident that it's safe to do so.

In this way, over many, many, MANY years, the caveperson's brain grew to be quite worried and cautious. This helped them to stay alive.

The world has changed a lot over the years. Think about it — when was the last time you found a tiger around the corner waiting to eat you? This probably hasn't happened to you any time recently! But our brains are still wired to think cautiously and worry.

Let's check how your brain works . . . there's a picture on the next page — don't turn it over yet! — but when you turn the page, I want you to

SHOUT OUT REALLY LOUDLY WHAT YOU SEE IN THE PICTURE.

The only rule is you can't stop and think about it. I want to know the first thing that comes into your mind.

READY?

3...

2...

1...

TURN THE PAGE

NOW!

WHAT DID YOU SHOUT OUT?

WAS IT 'SNAKE'?

100

The chances are that your brain first told you it was a snake, but if you slow down and take your time, you can probably now see it's a stick.

The first thought came from your 'caveperson-brain', trying to keep you safe.

SO STOP RIGHT THERE!

- ★ when you hit bumps and barriers
- ★ when you find it hard to try new things because you're worried you might fail
- ★ when things don't turn out how you wanted them to, and you feel like giving up

Because there's a good chance your inner caveperson might be overreacting. This part of our brain will see the worst in every situation and will sometimes confuse a bump in the road with a disaster.

This is completely normal, but realising this has happened is the first step towards switching tracks and getting back to your **LIMITLESS MINDSET.**

MENTAL MUSCLE ACTIVITY

Let's get to know your inner caveperson. Give them a name, draw a picture of them below and have some fun filling the speech bubbles in.

My inner caveperson is called

_____

They enjoy

_____

_____

_____

They worry about

_____

_____

_____

When setbacks happen they respond by thinking

_____

_____

_____

Hopefully you're starting to feel like you understand your caveperson-brain. It's a completely natural part of being you!

Now, I want you to show them how YOU want to think, feel and behave. This is really important, because to be the champion you truly are you need to dream big, challenge yourself, and make mistakes and learn from them . . . all things that the caveperson-brain worries about.

SO HOW DO YOU LOOK AFTER YOUR CAVEPERSON-BRAIN? ARE YOU READY FOR ANOTHER SIMPLE TRICK TO TRY OUT?

You might have noticed I always try to make these tricks spell out a simple word. This just helps me remember it. This one is the word **'CARE'**.

C = CONNECT

This means connecting with your caveperson-brain and **noticing** when they have something to say. This might be when you:

⭐ **Set a goal and the thought pops up 'but what if I'm not successful?', or you start to feel really unsure of yourself**

⭐ **Someone tells you that you can't do something and you think 'maybe they're right'**

⭐ **Think 'everyone will laugh at me' when you have a setback**

A = ACCEPT ITS NORMAL

★ Rather than worrying whether there's something wrong with you, this step means remembering that these thoughts and feelings are completely normal. Everyone has doubts. I do, your friends and family do, and even celebrities do.

★ Recognise that you don't need to fight with your doubts. You just need to show them a different way of thinking or behaving.

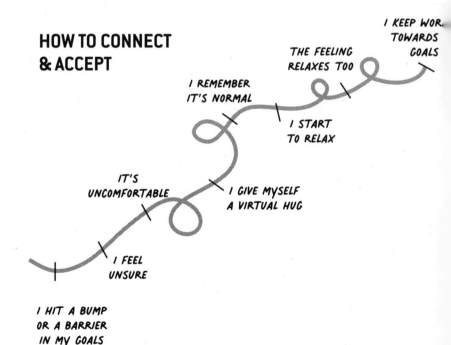

HOW TO CONNECT & ACCEPT

I KEEP WOR.
TOWARDS
GOALS

THE FEELING
RELAXES TOO

I REMEMBER
IT'S NORMAL

I START
TO RELAX

IT'S
UNCOMFORTABLE

I GIVE MYSELF
A VIRTUAL HUG

I FEEL
UNSURE

I HIT A BUMP
OR A BARRIER
IN MY GOALS

R = RETHINK

This step is all about **choosing how YOU want to think.**

When a thought from your caveperson-brain pops up, you could read
through the **Limitless Mindset** table on page 27, or talk to
yourself like you would a best friend. Or imagine someone from your
team is by your side giving you a pep talk — what would they say
to you? Even better, go and speak to one of them and tell them how
you're feeling.

Here's another idea . . . say that caveperson-brain thought out loud in the
voice of your favourite cartoon character. I like to do this in Donald Duck's
voice — it always makes me laugh!

WHEN WE PLAY WITH OUR DOUBTS AND WORRIES,
THEY SOMEHOW FEEL LESS POWERFUL. AND THEN
WE'RE MORE FREE TO KEEP FOLLOWING OUR DREAMS,
TAKE SOME RISKS AND KEEP MOVING FORWARD
AFTER A BUMP IN THE ROAD.

E = EXPERIMENT

The final step to move from caveperson-brain into a **LIMITLESS MINDSET** is to **do the thing you're worried about anyway.**

Confidence can come when you take this fourth step: when you experiment and leap out of your comfort zone, even when you're not feeling it, and see what happens. More often than not, it will go well. *AND IF IT DOESN'T . . . SO WHAT!*

You can learn to think positively, but that only lasts for so long. A more reliable way to finding your inner-champion is to accept your thoughts for what they are — just thoughts — and learn to step out there and do what you want, regardless of what's going on in your mind.

Whenever you move towards your hopes and dreams, bumps and barriers will naturally pop up. If you feel like giving up, I just want you to remember this one thing:

IF YOU KEEP GOING, ONE STEP AT A TIME, WHAT INITIALLY FELT IMPOSSIBLE WILL EVENTUALLY FEEL EASY. AND YOU'LL LOOK BACK ON HOW FAR YOU'VE COME AND YOU WILL BE AMAZED!

CELEBRATE

IT'S TIME TO TALK ABOUT THE IMPORTANCE OF CELEBRATING YOUR PROGRESS – BOTH THE SMALL STEPS AND THE BIG WINS!

Celebrating will help you to see how far you've come and be proud of the effort you've made. I have a friend who makes a list called *Good Things You Have Done* every year on 1 January. He adds to it bit-by-bit over the course of the year; sometimes adding things like the time he did something well at work, but also putting in smaller moments, like if he managed to beat me at a game of FIFA (this doesn't happen too often!). He has been doing this for years.

When I asked him why he makes this list of Good Things
year-after-year, he told me that his brain remembers
bad things happening in big, solid moments
and that they can take up a lot of space in his
head. But he also said that good things tend
to happen when loads of small things
go right over time, just like
the grains of sand

in an

h
o
u
r
glass.

When he adds good things to his list, he
is reminding himself of all of the little bits
that add up over time, so that when something
really amazing happens, he can remember
all of the little wins that got him to that place.

I thought that was a really useful way to think about life, so I started making small lists myself. Not just to remind me of the times when I've scored goals and won games, but also to remind myself of those smaller wins which helped get me to that point.

WHEN I TALK ABOUT 'WINS', I DON'T WANT YOU TO ONLY THINK ABOUT TIMES THAT YOU'VE WON A COMPETITION OR HAD A GOOD DAY AT SCHOOL.

The way I see it, if you've done some good in your day, that's a **win**. There is nothing too big or too small to be counted as a win, and your life is full of the tiny wins you achieve every single day.

THINGS YOU MIGHT NOT GET A GOLD MEDAL FOR, BUT THINGS THAT ARE DEFINITELY WORTH CELEBRATING NONETHELESS.

CONNECT THE DOTS

When you're busy living life, it can feel all a bit random.

We're always thinking about the future, thinking things like:

What should I do today?
What's happening tomorrow?

But it's really important to take the time to look back on all you've achieved and ask yourself:

What did I do well?
What am I proud of?
Who is proud of me?
What have I learnt?

When you do this, you can connect the dots and see all the small steps that led you to your goals and dreams — it will help you to think about what you've learnt and the people you want to thank. Plus, it's really good fun to do!

MENTAL MUSCLE ACTIVITY

THINK ABOUT SOMETHING YOU ARE PROUD OF AND WRITE IT DOWN BELOW. It could be something you have achieved, like making a sports team, passing an exam, or helping in your community – things that other people can see – or it could be something that only you know about, like getting through a tricky time or trying something you were scared of.

_____
_____
_____
_____
_____
_____
_____
_____
_____
_____

There is no such thing as an overnight success. When you see people being really successful, they have normally spent years and **YEARS** working hard to get there. Along the way they've had setbacks and they have struggled, but eventually, they've got to the place they wanted to go.

When I first started playing senior team football, there were a few people who described me as an 'overnight success' because I scored in my first game for Manchester United and for England. But that's not true. I had been training hard as a footballer for more than **10 YEARS** before I played in my first senior team match in 2016.

A LOT OF HARD WORK BEHIND THE SCENES WENT INTO THAT SUCCESS.

Behind all of your successes there will be lots of stepping stones (or dots) that you can only connect by looking back.

MY STEPPING STONES TO SCORING IN THOSE GAMES WERE THE SUPPORT FROM MY FAMILY AND FRIENDS, MAKING SURE I PRACTISED HARD AND LISTENING TO MY COACHES.

REMEMBER THAT THING YOU JUST WROTE DOWN THAT YOU'RE PROUD OF? CAN YOU THINK OF ALL THE LITTLE THINGS THAT HELPED YOU GET THERE? THINK REALLY CAREFULLY ABOUT THIS AND HAVE SOME FUN WITH IT! YOUR STEPPING STONES COULD INCLUDE:

★ Things you did on purpose to help you move in the right direction (like setting a goal, learning a new skill or learning from other people).

★ Random things that happened that helped you move in the right direction.

★ People who helped you along the way.

★ Things that went wrong, but that you learnt from.

★ Even tiny things, like making sure you were getting enough sleep so you were properly prepared and in the right place at the right time!

Now I want you to write down your stepping stones in the spaces below and as you do it, connect the dots to create your very own success picture!

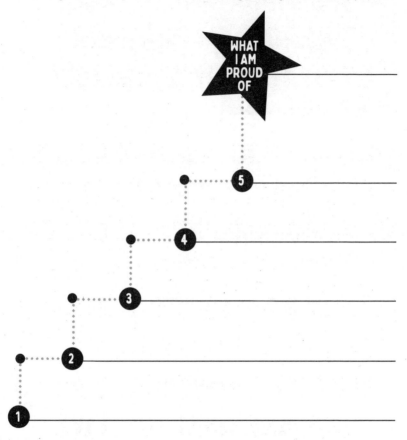

I hope you enjoyed connecting the dots and thinking about all the small steps that helped you get to that thing you're proud of. Every little step has contributed to where you ended up, so make sure you take the time to celebrate all of them!

IT'S IMPORTANT TO TAKE
TIME TO SLOW DOWN AND
ENJOY YOUR WINS, BECAUSE
SOMETIMES LIFE MOVES SO
QUICKLY YOU'LL WONDER HOW
EVERYTHING HAPPENED. IT CAN
BE IN OUR NATURE TO FOCUS ON
BIGGER AND BETTER THINGS,
AND ALWAYS WONDER 'WHAT'S
NEXT?' - BUT MAKE SURE YOU
APPRECIATE WHERE YOU ARE
NOW, AND WHAT YOU HAVE
DONE TO GET THERE.

Make a special effort to say thank you to all the people who have helped you follow your dreams so far, or even to thank the people who make you smile and help you get through the ups and downs of life. You could share your connect-the-dots picture with them, write them a short thank you note or just let them know how much you appreciate them.

As with all these activities, writing things down can really help you to think more clearly about how you got on and what you'd like to do going forward. Here are four sentences for you to have a go at completing before and after the activity:

1.   **I am going to say thank you to** . . . .
. . . .

2.   **I want them to know** . . . .
. . . .

3.   **Before doing this activity I felt** . . . .
. . . .

4.   **After doing this activity I felt** . . . .
. . . .

LOOKING AT WINS, EVEN AFTER A 'DEFEAT'

There will be days you can try your best and still lose. It can feel really tough to go out there, give 100% and still have things go wrong, but I want you to know that just because things didn't go the way you planned, it doesn't mean everything has gone wrong forever.

There are times when I tell myself:

> It's just a bad morning. It's not a bad day — you still have the afternoon to make it better.

OR

> It's just a bad day. It doesn't mean it has to be a bad week. If I put good energy and effort into things, I can fix it.

OR EVEN

> Ok, so that wasn't the best week, but what can I do to try and have a better one next week?

I had a football coach once tell me **'Don't draw the wrong conclusions from a bad result.'** Your team can play well and still lose, but that doesn't mean your team should stop doing all of the good things that got them to this point, just because they lost one game.

I try not to let a few bad days ruin my **LIMITLESS MINDSET**. In fact, there are times after a loss, or a mistake, when it's important to go through everything and look at things which went **RIGHT** so that

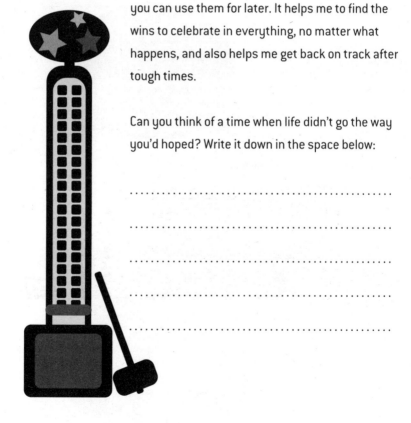

you can use them for later. It helps me to find the wins to celebrate in everything, no matter what happens, and also helps me get back on track after tough times.

Can you think of a time when life didn't go the way you'd hoped? Write it down in the space below:

....

....

....

....

....

Now I want you to think of **THREE WINS** you can celebrate from what you've written down. What went well? What did you learn? What can you try differently next time?

1. _____

   _____

2. _____

   _____

3. _____

   _____

THERE ARE WINS YOU CAN CELEBRATE IN EVERYTHING YOU DO. BELIEVE ME. AND WHEN YOU LEARN HOW TO CELEBRATE THOSE SMALLER WINS, YOU CAN USE THE ENERGY YOU GET FROM DOING THAT TO FOCUS ON WHAT YOU'D LIKE TO DO BETTER NEXT TIME.

So, for me, the ultimate measure of success is **BOTH** the effort you put in and the mindset you bring. If you get those things right over time, you'll probably get the results you want more often . . . but not always (that's just life). Sometimes you will try your best but come up short. Sometimes you will work hard and want something to happen, but you still won't get the result you want.

It's really tough when that happens, and when it happens to me I can feel quite down. To help myself feel more positive, I try to remember these important points:

 Celebrate the effort you put in

 Ask yourself: what would it take for me to get the result I want?

 Ask people I trust for their ideas

 Go again!

And I try **not** to buy in or believe thoughts like these:

 I am a failure

 I should be embarrassed

 People will think badly of me

Our thoughts are really powerful, but when they're negative it can almost be like someone has a megaphone in your brain telling you unhelpful things. I try to remember that thoughts are not facts – you can't see them or touch them!

Ask yourself 'Is thinking this way helping me move towards my goals?' If the answer is no, then you need to **switch mindset.**

Responding like this takes a bit of skill, but if you practise over time, it will get easier.

Remember your inner caveperson brain? Well, sometimes they're in such a rush to work out what's happening that they miss some of the detail. Here's an example. As quick as you can, read what's in the circles below:

HOT
IN THE
THE SUMMER

ONCE
IN A
A LIFETIME

SHOE
ON THE
THE FOOT

Hot in the summer, right?

Now I want you to read it again really slowly. Pay attention to every single word.

When you do this, you'll notice there are two 'the's' and two 'a's'. Most people don't expect to see the extra word so our brains take it out!

Here's another brain teaser. Read the sentence below and count how many times you see the letter **F** or **f**.

Finished files are the result of years of scientific study combined with the experience of years.

How many did you get?

Most people count three but in fact there are six. We often forget to include the fs in the word 'of'. This is partly because the letter f usually makes the 'f' sound like in 'field'. In the word 'of', it makes a 'v' sound. Plus, you're probably so used to seeing the word 'of' that you process it as one unit and overlook the second letter.

It's the same for how we think about life, and particularly how we reflect on our efforts. **Sometimes we see things that aren't really there.** Sometimes we miss things all together — maybe you hadn't realised how close you are to getting the results you want — or we see things differently to how they actually are — for example, you might think you've failed when in fact you've tried your best, and still achieved something amazing. So, when you take time to connect the dots or make your own measure of success, you're able to see things a lot more clearly. To let the lake settle and allow the big brilliant fish at the bottom to swim to the surface.

Here's another way of thinking about it:

HOW WE'RE TAUGHT TO MEASURE SUCCESS:

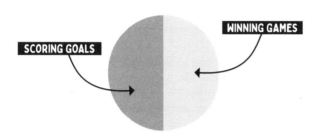

BUT A BETTER MEASURE WOULD BE:

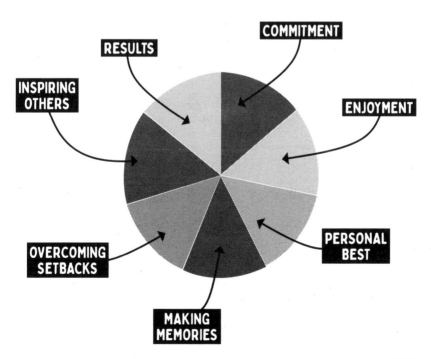

So, if you're sitting there wondering how to celebrate success when you haven't quite achieved the result you wanted, here's what I want you to do:

★ Make your own measure of success: imagine this like a pizza with different slices. Only one slice can be about the results

★ Have a go at labelling the different slices in the pizza opposite

★ If you're not sure, here are some of the ones that I use:

  ✦ **Prepare well**

  ✦ **Get ideas from my team**

  ✦ **Try my best in the moment**

  ✦ **Keep trying when things go wrong**

  ✦ **Have fun no matter what**

  ✦ **Learn useful stuff**

★ Colour in the ones that you achieved

★ Write down three steps you could take to be able to colour in the blank slices

MY MEASURES OF SUCCESS:

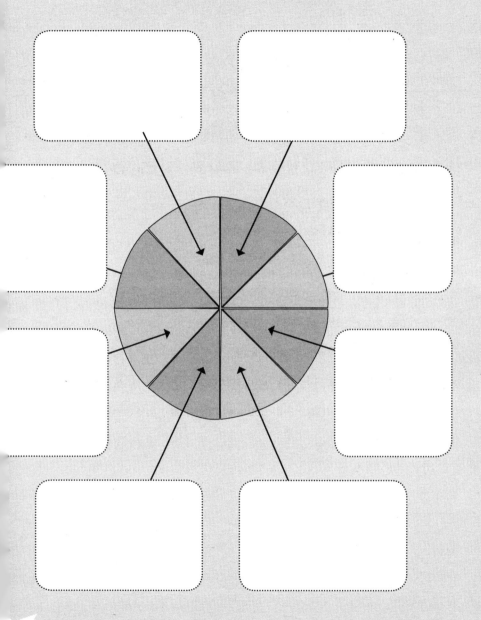

When you're working towards achieving your dreams, chances are you're going to fall short from time to time.

But nothing is ever a complete failure, and you can always turn it around.

When you feel disappointed about the way something has gone, I want you to use your **MENTAL MUSCLE** to see the ways in which you were successful, and be proud of them. I also want you to use your **MENTAL MUSCLE** to see the ways in which you weren't successful, and use these as opportunities to learn.

When you do this, you can bring yourself back to a LIMITLESS MINDSET.

CONCLUSION

We're nearly at the end of our journey together – I hope you've enjoyed exploring your hopes and dreams, working on your mindset and building your skills. **We've come a long way!**

1. Find our dream
2. Mindset matters
3. Fuel your adventures
4. Build your team
5. Success and setbacks
6. Celebrate

NOW IT'S TIME FOR SOME FINAL IDEAS TO TURBOCHARGE YOUR JOURNEY.

1. REMEMBER: THIS IS ABOUT YOU

You are completely unique and your journey is yours and only yours. No one can be you as well as **YOU** can be you! I hope that this book has helped you find ways to unlock some of the amazing ideas you already have within you. Some of them might not work out — but remember that every time something doesn't work out, you're closer to finding the next idea that will — some of them might still be half-baked, and some might change the world.

> **FROM SMALL GOALS TO BIG DREAMS, GIVE YOURSELF TIME TO UNCOVER YOUR TRUE THOUGHTS.**

Not just your caveperson thoughts, but the big and exciting thoughts that only come to the top when you slow down and spend some time with yourself, daring to dream big.

If you ever get the chance, I hope you come back to this book at a later date and add to all of the activities you've done and watch how your feelings have changed. Remember, there might be a lot of people out there with the same book as you, but no one is going to have all of the same stuff that is inside **THIS** book.

THIS BOOK IS ABOUT YOU, AND ONLY YOU CAN MAKE IT **YOUR OWN.**

2. YOUR POTENTIAL IS LIMITLESS

You have the most amazing machine in the world between your ears. It has 100 billion neurons, which is about the same as the number of stars in the Milky Way galaxy.

Information runs between these neurons at 250mph, which is about the same speed as the fastest car in the world. It weighs just 2% of your total body weight, yet it uses around 25% of the energy you get from food every day. It generates up to 25 watts of electricity, which is enough to power a light bulb, and contains 2,500,000 GB of storage space – the top-of-the-line iPhone has 56.

You've probably worked it out by now – but just in case – **I'M TALKING ABOUT YOUR BRAIN!** And most amazing of all, every time you complete one of the **MENTAL MUSCLE** activities in this workbook, you make your brain stronger. That means you'll be able to do more and more cool stuff in your life.

3. YOU ARE ENOUGH, JUST AS YOU ARE

SPECIAL   **SPECIAL**

In this book I've encouraged you to work on your mindset and follow your dreams – just like my mum, my siblings and my coaches have encouraged me over the years. But I just need to make one thing really clear – I'm not encouraging you because you're not enough as you are. In life, it's easy to fall into the trap of thinking that you are only special if you achieve big things, look a certain way or hang out with certain people.

This isn't true.

The truth is, you are special and enough, just as you are. Nothing will ever change that, no matter what happens. Nothing that anyone says about you or thinks about you can change that.

> *SO, FOLLOW YOUR DREAMS AND STRIVE TO BE THE BEST YOU CAN BE BECAUSE IT'S FUN AND AMAZING, NOT BECAUSE YOU THINK YOU'RE NOT ENOUGH AS YOU ARE.*

143

4. YOU ARE NOT A ROBOT

Throughout this book we've talked about the difference between a **LIMITED MINDSET** and a **LIMITLESS MINDSET**. Let's recap a few pointers:

LIMITED MINDSET

- The result defines you
- You try to impress others
- Everyone's opinion matters

LIMITLESS MINDSET

- Your effort and attitude define you
- You try to impress yourself
- The only opinions that matter are those of the people who you seek advice from

Remember, no one can be in a **LIMITLESS MINDSET** all the time, so go easy on yourself. You want to be your biggest fan whenever you can, rather than your biggest critic.

What we think doing our best looks like:

What doing our best actually looks like:

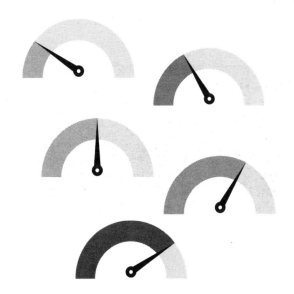

So, rather than trying to be a robot, the real key to success is to focus on doing the best you can, with the skills you have, in the situation you find yourself in. This will look slightly different each day, depending on what's going on, how you've slept and how you're feeling – and that's ok.

5. LIFE IS NOT BLACK AND WHITE

On your journey to be the best you can be, you might start to notice that there's no one way to be human. In fact, sometimes you might find yourself feeling things that feel like complete opposites! For example, you can be:

- **A champion and still fail**

- **A hard worker and need a break**

- **A strong person and need support**

- **Trying to work on your mindset, but also sometimes just want to play computer games**

In these moments, I find it really helps to ask myself one simple question:

*'What advice would I give a best friend
who was in this situation?'*

This question works again and again and again for me. It helps me think more clearly and work out what to do. So, if you find that you are second-guessing yourself or unsure, ask yourself what advice the mini Marcus in your pocket might give you, and go from there.

I hope you've enjoyed thinking about your dreams and working on your mindset. You've made a **BIG** commitment to building your **MENTAL MUSCLE**, and you should be so proud of that. The more you do this, the more you'll find yourself in a **LIMITLESS MINDSET**, and that is an incredible thing – because when you think of a life with no limits, there's nothing you can't do!

GOOD LUCK ON YOUR ADVENTURES. I CAN'T WAIT TO SEE WHAT YOU DO NEXT.

REMEMBER – THERE ARE NO LIMITS ON WHAT YOU ARE CAPABLE OF.

UNTIL NEXT TIME!

M.R.

ABOUT THE AUTHORS

Marcus Rashford MBE

Marcus Rashford MBE is Manchester United's iconic number 10 and an England International footballer.

During the lockdown imposed due to the COVID-19 pandemic, Marcus teamed up with the food distribution charity FareShare to cover the free school meal deficit for vulnerable children across the UK, raising in excess of £20 million pounds. Marcus successfully lobbied the British Government to U-turn policy around the free food voucher programme – a campaign that has been deemed the quickest turnaround of government policy in the history of British politics – so that 1.3 million vulnerable children continued to have access to food supplies whilst schools were closed during the pandemic.

In response to Marcus's End Child Food Poverty campaign, the British Government committed £400 million to support vulnerable children across the UK, supporting 1.7 million children for the next 12 months. In October 2020, he was appointed MBE in the Queen's Birthday Honours. Marcus has committed himself to combating child poverty in the UK and his books *You Are a Champion* and its follow up *You Can Do It* are inspiring guides for children, about reaching their full potential. He is also the author of *The Breakfast Club Adventures;* an exciting, highly-illustrated adventure inspired by Marcus's own experiences growing up.

Katie Warriner

Katie is one of the UK's leading Performance Psychologists, working in diverse settings, from the sports field to the boardroom, the helicopter pad to the operating theatre. Her clients include CEOs, Olympic Champions, professional sports teams and educational leaders.

She recently co-founded the Moonshot Series, alongside Jenna Ashford to deliver world-class mindset training in schools and youth settings. Through their pioneering mindset course, SPARK, they are on a mission to empower young people to explore their potential and learn critical skills to manage life's ups and downs.

Prior to this, Katie was embedded within Team GB, supporting many of the most successful athletes and coaches at the London 2012, Rio 2016 and Tokyo 2022 Olympic Games. Above all, Katie is passionate about supporting people to be the best they can be and to live their life with purpose.

Katie lives in Leamington Spa with her husband and their daughter.

Carl Anka

Carl Anka is a London-born journalist and broadcaster who likes his tea with milk and one sugar. He has written for the *BBC*, *The Guardian, VICE, NME, GQ* and *BuzzFeed* among other publications online and in print, and specialises in writing about pop culture, video games, films and football. Currently a reporter for sports media group *The Athletic*, covering Manchester United, he is the host of the *Talk of the Devils* podcast and is scared of talking on the phone.

Along with Marcus Rashford, Carl is the co-writer of *You Are a Champion* and its follow up *You Can Do It* – positive and inspiring guides for life for young readers.

REFERENCES

Chapter 1

Wilson TD, Reinhard DA, Westgate EC, Gilbert DT, Ellerbeck N, Hahn C, Brown CL, Shaked A. Social psychology. *Just think: the challenges of the disengaged mind.* Science (2014).

Chapter 3

Black, T. D. (2022). *Act for Treating Children: The Essential Guide to Acceptance and Commitment Therapy for Kids*. New Harbinger Publications.

Chapter 4

Triple H exercise as featured in *The Power of a Positive Team: Proven Principles and Practices that Make Great Teams Great* by Jon Gordon. Wiley (2018).

Chapter 6

How we're taught to measure success, as featured on The Prime Clinic Instagram, @theprime_clinic, Leamington Spa (2022).

THE MARCUS RASHFORD BOOK CLUB

Look out for the Marcus Rashford Book Club logo – it's on books Marcus thinks you'll love!

A brilliantly illustrated, laugh-out-loud, wacky adventure through time!

Marcus says: 'The perfect story to escape into and find adventure. Pooja is super talented and I'm a big fan!'

Meet the Dream Defenders! They're on a mission to banish your worries while you sleep!

TOM PERCIVAL

'I would have loved this book as a child' Marcus Rashford MBE

Silas AND THE Marvellous Misfits

A fantastic DREAM DEFENDERS adventure!

Marcus says: 'Fun, engaging, action-packed – I would have loved this book as a child!'

Marcus says: 'Breakfast Club is about forming friendships, about togetherness, about escape. It was where some of my greatest memories were made. I want to capture that feeling in my debut fiction book.'

Andy and Terry live in the world's BEST treehouse! A hilariously wacky adventure told through text and fantastic cartoon-style illustrations!

Marcus says: 'It's the perfect combination of wacky adventure and illustration, and I'm sure you're going to love it. I did!'

THE MARCUS RASHFORD BOOK CLUB

The Marcus Rashford Book Club is a collaboration between Marcus Rashford MBE and Macmillan Children's Books, helping children aged 8–12 to develop literacy as a life skill and a love of reading. Two books will be chosen each year by Marcus and the Macmillan team, one in summer and another in the autumn, with the mission to increase children's access to books outside of school. The book club will feature an exciting selection of titles, which aim to make every child feel supported, represented and empowered.

The book club launched in June 2021, with the fully illustrated, laugh-out-loud, time-travel adventure, *A Dinosaur Ate My Sister* by Pooja Puri, illustrated by Allen Fatimaharan, followed by *Silas and the Marvellous Misfits* by Tom Percival, an action-packed, fully-illustrated adventure that shows kids the joy of being themselves. Marcus's own book, *The Breakfast Club Adventures: The Beast Beyond the Fence*, written with Alex Falase-Koya, was the third book in the club, and the fourth is *The 13-Storey Treehouse* by Andy Griffiths and Terry Denton. Copies of these books will be available in shops, and to ensure all children have access to them, free copies will also be distributed to support under-privileged and vulnerable children across the UK.

Don't miss Marcus Rashford's positive and inspiring guides for life!

The Number One Bestseller

OUT NOW!

'I want to show you how you can be a champion in almost anything you put your mind to.'

Marcus Rashford MBE is famous worldwide for his skills both on and off the pitch - but before he was a Manchester United and England footballer, and long before he started his inspiring campaign to end child food poverty, he was just an ordinary kid from Wythenshawe, South Manchester. Now the nation's favourite footballer wants to show YOU how to achieve your dreams, in this positive and inspiring guide for life.

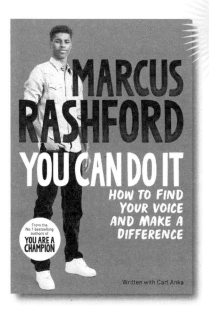

'One person isn't going to change the world, but your voice can make a huge difference.'

Marcus uses the power of his voice to shine a light on the injustices that he cares passionately about, and now he wants to help YOU find the power in yours! From surrounding yourself with the right team, to showing kindness to those around you, to celebrating and championing difference, Marcus shows you that your voice really does matter and that you can do anything you put your mind to. Even the smallest changes can have the biggest impact.

Don't miss Marcus Rashford's first fiction book for kids!

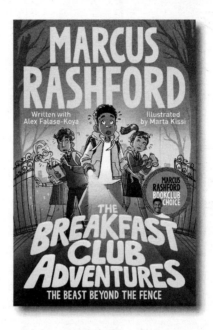

There's something strange going on at school . . .

When twelve-year-old Marcus kicks his favourite football over the school fence, he knows he's never getting it back. Nothing that goes over that wall **ever** comes comes back.

But when Marcus gets a mysterious note inviting him to join The Breakfast Club Investigators he is soon pulled into an exciting adventure to solve the mystery, along with his new mates Stacey, Lise and Asim!

As they uncover one surprising clue after another, the Breakfast Club Investigators start to realize that things aren't as they seem, and there might be something strange lurking just beyond the fence . . .